Sports Illustrated
GOLF

The Sports Illustrated Library

Sports Illustrated
GOLF

By CHARLES PRICE
and the Editors of
Sports Illustrated

J. B. LIPPINCOTT COMPANY
Philadelphia and New York

U.S. Library of Congress Cataloging in Publication Data

Price, Charles, birth date
   Sports illustrated golf.

   (The Sports illustrated library)
   First ed. by the editors of Sports illustrated and C.
Price published under title: Sports illustrated book of golf.
   1. Golf. I. Sports illustrated (Chicago) II. Title.
III. Title: Sports illustrated book of golf.
GV965.P74 1972   796.352   72-4143
ISBN-0-397-00937-2
ISBN-0-397-00938-0 (pbk.)

Copyright © 1970, 1972, by Time Inc.

Printed in the United States of America

Revised Edition

10 9 8

Photographs from *Sports Illustrated*, © Time Inc.

Cover photograph: Don Bender

Photographs on pages 8, 19, 31, 32, 44, 82, 38 and 86: United Press International

Photographs on pages 12-13 and 38-39: Lizabeth Corlett, DPI

Photograph on page 18: Walter Iooss, Jr., S.I.

Photograph on page 26: Wayne Wilson, Leviton-Atlanta

Photograph on page 85: Eric Schweikardt, S.I.

Contents

Illustrations by Frank Mullins

Sports Illustrated

1
The Game and the Course

THERE is little or no point in taking up the game of golf unless you realize from the start what an appallingly diffi cult game it is to play well. The technique of hitting a golf ball, the mastery of which is still no guarantee of playing good golf, involves almost every part of the body—the feet, the legs, the hips, the shoulders, the arms, the hands, even the head—all coordinated to a near preposterously fine degree.

After twenty five years of playing golf, several of them as the game's leading money winner, the incomparably methodical Ben Hogan took apart his swing and put it back together in somewhat different form, to everyone's astonishment, it actually turned out to be an improvement.

At forty, and with a national championship already under his belt, professional Jay Hebert declared he was still not altogether satisfied with his grip, the most rudimentary aspect of physical golf.

For years one of the most technically perfect swingers of a golf club has been a Philadelphia professional named George Fazio, a former Canadian Open champion who lost the 1950 National Open in a play-off with Hogan. At the age of fifty-four and with his golfing interests now directed almost entirely to architecture, Fazio belatedly discovered how he could make his shoulders and his hips turn in the proper ratio, which is approximately 2 to 1; that is to say, with the shoulders turning twice as far as the hips on the backswing. Fazio found that he could maintain this ratio simply by holding his right knee as steady as possible. On such simplicities are golf secrets promulgated.

While the act of hitting the ball is intricate enough, it is nevertheless only a part of the complexness of golf. There is a distressing degree of luck in the game to boot. Golfers often hit a shot exactly as intended only to have the ball bury in a bunker, while a terribly mis-hit ball might roll miraculously into the cup. And everybody has had the experience of playing well only to lose a match and the equally baffling experience of playing badly only to win one. In a professional career that covered nearly forty years, the great Walter Hagen managed to make only a single hole-in-one, yet there are 90-shooters who have made a half a dozen. How do you explain?

To eliminate the chaos into which the element of chance might very well throw the game, the United States Golf Association in collaboration with the Royal and Ancient Golf Club of St. Andrews, Scotland, has promulgated forty-one Rules of Play and thirty-four Definitions of terms peculiar to golf, plus an appendix covering everything from the proper dimensions for flagsticks to the legal markings on iron clubs. These are published in a booklet that hardly anybody ever bothers to read and almost nobody thoroughly understands.

To the casual golfer, who seldom plays any other golf course but his own, the Rules seem to be a masterpiece of circumlocution. Yet, when you consider that no two courses are alike and that a single course seldom plays the same way two days running, the Rules are almost all-encompassing for the incredible number of situations that can arise in a game that is played in almost as many countries as there are United Nations. Thus, a Rule that purposefully grew out of a situation that arose on a course hard by the sea in Scotland centuries ago will adequately cover a situation that might arise on a course tomorrow high in the Chilean Andes. It will because each of them is based on the unwritten rule upon which golf has been played since it began: play the ball as it lies and the course as you find it.

The word "golf" is derived from the Germanic word *kolbe,* which means simply "club." Beyond the origin of its name, the game is entirely Scottish in character, although there have been arguments to the contrary. One of these arguments is that the game was originally Dutch, a supposition that is supported by innumerable pictures by old masters depicting the Dutch playing games that bear some similarity to golf but a good deal more similarity to some form of hockey, the oldest game in the world.

These diatribes notwithstanding, we do know that golf was played in Scotland five and a half centuries ago and we do *not* know that it was played anywhere else. Whatever games might have been played elsewhere, we are aware that nearly six centuries ago it was the Scots who first combined in a game the characteristics of hitting a ball cross-country with a variety of implements to a hole in the ground without interference by an opponent. That's real golf, and no other game is quite like it.

A round of golf consists of eighteen holes played in their correct sequence. This is to say that, unless otherwise stipulated by a committee before a tournament round, they must be played from the first through the eighteenth in the order they appear on a scorecard. No other sequence is legally a "round" of golf. It is, therefore, not proper to play the second nine holes before playing the first nine and still

consider your score official for such things as determining a "handicap," the system, unique to golf among all games, whereby you can play golf on even terms tomorrow anywhere with anybody, not excluding Jack Nicklaus.

The expression "hole" has both a general and a specific use in golf. Specifically, it is a cup 4¼ inches in diameter sunk at least 4 inches below the surface of the ground. Into it is stuck a "flagstick."

While a flagstick almost invariably has a flag attached to it, usually with a numeral on it indicating the correct number of the hole, it does not have to. Merion, a famous championship course near Philadelphia, has wicker baskets attached to its flagsticks rather than actual bunting. So long as it is a movable, straight, round indicator centered in the hole to show its position, however, it is a flagstick. And there are Rules that apply to its use.

Speaking *generally*, a hole is also the entire area from the teeing ground, off which play begins, through the green to the putting surface in which the specific hole, or cup, has been placed, marked, as noted, with a flagstick.

The "teeing ground" is the starting place for the hole to be played. It is usually an elongated flat surface with turf mowed to a fine consistency. That part of it from which the hole may be legally played is a rectangular area two clublengths in depth, the front and the sides of which are defined by two markers, usually plastic balls about the size of grapefruits.

The golf ball is usually placed upon a "tee," a wooden peg about the length of a toothpick. (The term "tee" is almost invariably used also as a diminutive for "teeing ground.") The ball may not be placed in front of the outside limits of the markers. Neither may it be placed behind the markers by more than two clublengths, that measurement to be determined by the length of the club you are using on the hole. However, you may *stand* outside these limits.

The ball is put into play when it is fairly struck from this

14

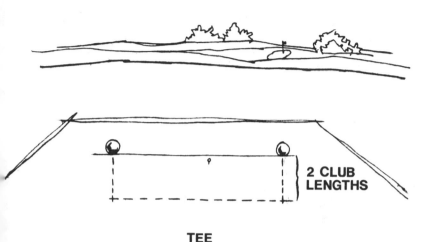

TEE

The teeing ground—or "tee," for short—is the area from which play begins on each hole.

area. It is not considered to have been struck fairly should you accidentally knock the ball off its tee while addressing it.

On each hole there are usually three sets of markers: blue, white and yellow, although there may be exceptions to these colors. (Golf is full of exceptions, most of which, for the sake of sanity, you might just as well ignore.) The blue markers are usually placed at or near the extreme back of the teeing ground, thereby stretching the course to its ultimate, or championship, length, which today could be 7000 yards or more. The white tees are set considerably in front of the blues, shortening the course to, let's say, 6500 yards.

15

These are the ones most men ought, and will want, to play. Farther in front of the white markers will be the red, which are meant for ladies and which diminish the course to, say, an even 6000 yards.

In a match, the order of who is to play first off the tee, regardless of the color of the markers, is determined by "honor." He who plays off the tee of the *first* hole holds the honor until someone else scores a hole in fewer strokes, whereupon he loses the honor to that player.

From the tee, the ball is played toward the hole "through the green." Strictly speaking, this expression means the whole area of the course with the exceptions of the tee off which you have just played, hazards, and the putting surface into which the hole has been placed, there being special Rules that apply to all these exceptions.

Although not spelled out in the Rules of Golf, "through the green" is universally accepted to consist of two separate areas: "fairway" and "rough." Fairway is turf that has been mowed to a lawn-like consistency. Playing shots off it seldom presents a problem, and the direction of its sweep from the tee is almost invariably the easiest and most judicious way to eventually reach the putting surface.

Rough, on the other hand, is turf that has been allowed to grow to a coarse consistency, often several inches in height. Additionally, it may contain stones, rocks, bushes, even trees, playing from or around which can be difficult, if not impossible.

"Hazards" may lie within either the confines of the fairway or the rough, although they are usually bordered at least by the latter. They come in two forms: "bunker" and "water."

A bunker is an area of ground, barren of grass, that is usually covered with sand. Bunkers, which almost always are referred to as "sand traps," come in an unlimited variety of shapes and sizes. Indeed, the contouring of them is considered one of the major talents of a golf course architect. Some bunkers are no wider than a barrel, others are the size

16

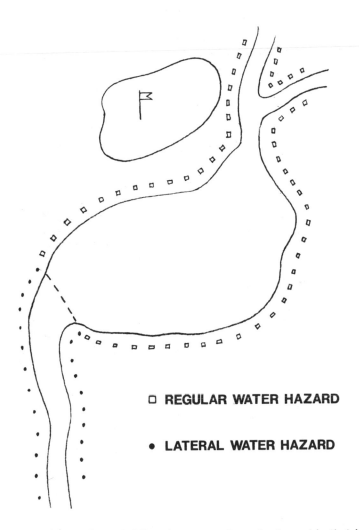

☐ **REGULAR WATER HAZARD**

● **LATERAL WATER HAZARD**

A lateral water hazard differs from a regular water hazard in that it runs approximately parallel to the line of play. Since it cannot be kept between you and the hole when you drop the ball at a penalty of one stroke, you are permitted to drop it within two clublengths of the hazard but not nearer the hole.

of a backyard swimming pool, and still some others have been known to cover acres.

A "water hazard" is any sea, lake, pond, river, ditch or any other natural channel through which water runs, even though that channel might be temporarily drained of water. A ball played into it must be dropped somewhere behind the point of entry with a penalty of one stroke, should you choose not to play the ball, an improbable situation under the luckiest of circumstances.

A "lateral" water hazard (often mistakenly referred to as "parallel") is a water hazard, or part of one, running approximately parallel to the line of play and so situated that it is impracticable to drop the ball behind the water along the line of entry while still keeping it between the player and the hole. The penalty here is again one stroke, providing the ball is dropped no farther than two clublengths from the hazard and not nearer the hole.

All hazards, whether bunker or water, carry a concomitant number of exceptional Rules. Chief among them is a penalty for grounding your club as you address the ball in recovering from the hazard, the theory behind this Rule being that you would, intentionally or not, thereby be testing the texture of the sand or the depth of the water from which you are trying to extricate the ball.

The eventual target on every hole, of course, is the cup. But the immediate target as you play down the fairway or from the rough or out of hazards is the putting green in which the cup has been placed. Playing the ball directly into the cup from off the putting green does not happen without a degree of skill, to be sure. But neither does it happen also without a high degree of luck. Therefore, logic dictates that your objective be the putting green rather than the cup itself, the closer you can get it to the cup the better, all the while keeping in mind that hazards make discretion the better part of valor.

A ball 30 feet from the cup on the putting surface is inarguably a shot that has been played more soundly than a ball half that distance lying in a bunker. Once, on a crucial hole in a tight match for the British Amateur Championship, the great Bobby Jones purposely hit a long second shot 60 feet off line to the flagstick in order to avoid a tiny bunker that was directly in its line and not 20 feet from it. Although desperately trying to win the hole from his opponent, he knew from his vast experience that any shot on or near the putting surface, regardless of its length, would be wiser than one in that bunker. While Jones did not win the hole, he did not lose it either. Two holes later, he closed out the match and eventually went on to win the title and make his unparalleled Grand Slam—the Open and Amateur Championships of both the United States and Great Britain in a single season. Looking back, he still considers his decision to avoid that bunker at all costs one of the most intelligent he made among the many he had to make in order to fulfill that unforgettable golfing season.

The "putting green" is all ground specially prepared for putting, sometimes mowed to ⁹⁄₁₆ inch. Putting is the ultimate sophistication of golf playing. It is accomplished with a very short club whose face has little or no loft, thereby allowing the ball to be rolled rather than lofted. Putting surfaces, particularly on a championship course, can be awesomely immense, mystifyingly contoured and fantastically well-groomed. There are greens wider than a football field, greens that drop the height of a house from back to front, greens that are slicker than a hot tin roof. Jones once sank a putt at St. Andrews, Scotland, more than 60 yards long. Walter Hagen, the great professional after World War I, once stroked a putt on a green so fast that it rolled out of bounds, or clear off the confines of the golf course.

A round of golf has not always been set at eighteen holes. To discover just how the figure of eighteen was arrived at— and not ten or twelve or twenty—requires a dip into history. Beginning in 1744, golf began to be informally ruled by The Honourable Company of Edinburgh Golfers, a group that then played at the nearby Links of Leith, which is no longer in existence and which now plays at Muirfield, about a forty-five-minute drive east of Edinburgh. At the time, Leith had only five holes, although it was eventually lengthened to seven, and a round of golf was set at any random figure. Since golf then was always played in head-to-head matches, it made little difference what number of holes a round was, so long as the number was established before play began.

Then, beginning with a set of rules it laid down in 1754, a group that called itself The Society of St. Andrews Golfers and played its golf on the other side of the Firth of Forth, 33 miles northeast of Edinburgh, slowly began to take over the leadership of the game. (They are known today as the Royal and Ancient Golf Club of St. Andrews, Scotland.) At that time, St. Andrews had twelve holes. In a round, however, ten of these holes were played in duplicate. You started by playing eleven straight holes, then turned around and played ten of the same holes backward, finishing the round by playing a solitary hole near where you had started. Thus, a complete round at St. Andrews consisted of twenty-two holes.

In 1764, however, the Society combined four of the holes into two. Since these holes were duplicated in the course of play, a round at St. Andrews was thus reduced from twenty-two holes to eighteen, a number that came to be accepted as standard as the influence of St. Andrews spread.

That influence in golf the world over has been enormous. St. Andrews not only established golf as an eighteen-hole game but, by spelling out that set of rules in 1754, formed the basic theories for the Rules we use to this day. Additionally, many years before, it was at St. Andrews that caddies first came into use. The term "caddie" is derived from the French word *cadet*, meaning younger brother or son. The word undoubtedly came into use in Scotland in reference to the children of the French nobility who formed much of the court of Mary Queen of Scots, who resided

22

in St. Andrews. In time, the term began to be applied to errand boys and porters, some of whom were employed at times to carry clubs under their arms for the many noblemen who played and to clear the way for an advancing match through the pandemonium that existed on the links in those days.

The golf links then had the status of public parks and were overrun with sheep, cows, and hordes of rabbits. As protection against the biting winds that blew in off the sea, these animals often burrowed holes in the ground that soon filled with sand from the adjoining beaches. Hence, the formation of sand bunkers as an integral hazard of golf. Since the links were open to the public, they often became the scene for such spectacles as horse racing, cricket matches, and cattle shows. They were also apt to be populated at any time by soldiers drilling, washerwomen bleaching their linen, fishermen drying their nets, housewives beating carpets, children playing games and nurses sunning babies. It was one of a caddie's duties to clear the way through it all for golf players and to find and mark the hole with a gull's feather, the idea of flagsticks not having yet occurred to anyone.

St. Andrews is historically considered to be the classic golf course—a seaside links. While all golf links are golf courses, in purely technical terms, not all golf courses are golf links. A links is a golf course built on linksland, the sandy deposits by the sea left by centuries of receding oceanic tides. All but treeless, windblown, rainswept, they are considered the ultimate test of a man playing golf under heroic weather conditions. By tradition, all British championships are played over them, some of the more famous being (in addition to St. Andrews) Muirfield, Carnoustie and Troon in Scotland and Hoylake, Birkdale and Sandwich in England. Genuine links are rare in the United States.

Every hole on a golf course falls into one of three categories: par-three, par-four, or par-five. With an allowance

23

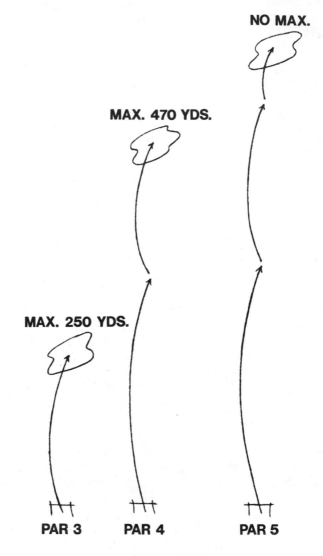

NO MAX.

MAX. 470 YDS.

MAX. 250 YDS.

PAR 3   PAR 4   PAR 5

PAR FOR A HOLE

Par for a hole is basically established by its yardage. It implies faultless play and two putts per green.

being made for two strokes on each putting green, par is the score that an expert golfer would be expected to make on each of those holes. It implies playing without error and without any accidental strokes of luck. Theoretically, then, on a par-three you are expected to hit the putting green in a single stroke off the tee and take two putts. On a par-four, you are expected to reach the putting green in two strokes. And on a par-five, reach it in three.

The basic guide for computing the par for a hole is its length in yardage, although its configuration and the severity of its hazards have some bearing. The yardage of a hole is measured, on the flat, from the middle of its tee area through mid-fairway to a point halfway from the front edge of the putting green to its back edge. A par-three hole is any hole up to 250 yards long. A par-four is any hole longer than that up to 470 yards. A par-five is any hole longer than *that*. (For women, these yardages run anywhere from 40 to 70 yards less.) The total of all the different pars adds up to par for the course. Most modern courses have a total par of 72, consisting of ten par-fours, four par-fives, and four par-threes. However, there are any number of courses where par might be 71 or 70, and courses with par as low as 69 or as high as 73 are not unheard of.

While par implies errorless play without flukes, you may arrive at it any way you can. Nothing in the Rules of Golf states how you must arrive at it. The nature of the game is not *how*, but *how many*. Thus, you may make a par by missing the green in the regulation number of strokes but then take only one putt—or no putts. You not only may make a par in this fashion, you more than likely will.

While par also implies perfect play, it may often in fact be surpassed. You may play a hole in one stroke less than par, in which case you have scored, in the parlance of the game, a "birdie." You may play a hole in two strokes less than par. On a par-three, this score is referred to as a "hole-in-one," the ultimate thrill in golf. On a par-four or a par-

25

five, this score is referred to as an "eagle." You may even play a hole in three strokes less than par; say, a par-five in two strokes. This score is referred to as a "double-eagle," and is very rare. In fact, playing a par-four in three strokes less than par—a hole-in-one, really—has happened on rare occasions.

Conversely—and much more likely—you may play a hole in one over par, a score that is referred to as a "bogey." Two over par is referred to as a "double-bogey." All higher scores in golf for some reason go nameless, mainly because they are regarded as unspeakable and, when made, unprintable.

The game of golf is played in two basic forms: "match" and "stroke." (The latter is usually erroneously referred to as "medal.") Each form of play has its own specific Rules. Stroke play is the form most widely used by professionals. The British Amateur Championship, which is sponsored by the Royal and Ancient Golf Club, is the only major national championship still played under the Rules of match.

In stroke play the competitor who holes the stipulated round or rounds in the fewest strokes is the winner. In match play the game is played by holes, one "side" against another. A side may be only a solitary player, but it may also be a group of two or more players, who are referred to as partners.

A hole is won by the side which holes its ball in the fewer strokes. A hole is said to be "halved" if each side holes out in the same number of strokes. A match is won by the side which is leading by a number of holes greater than the number of holes remaining to be played. Matches are usually played at eighteen holes, although sometimes they are played at thirty-six.

One popular but unofficial form of match-play competition is known as a "Nassau." This consists of three matches in one. One point is allotted for the first nine holes, another point for the second nine holes, and another point for the over-all eighteen. Thus, if you were to win the front nine

1 up and then lose the back nine 1 down, the over-all eighteen-hole match would have been halved.

The most popular manner of match play consists of one player against another. This, strictly speaking, is known as a "single," although the expression is hardly ever used. Golfers usually just refer to it as a match.

A "threesome" is a match in which one plays against two, each side playing one ball, the team of two playing alternate shots.

A "foursome" is a match in which two play against two, each side playing one ball in alternate strokes. This is an antiquated form of competition and is hardly ever used except in competitions between teams of mixed sex; say, a man and his wife. The term "foursome" is informally used to refer to any group of four players together playing any form of competition they wish.

A "three-ball" is a match in which three play against one another, each playing his own ball.

A "best-ball" is a match in which one plays against the better ball of two or the best ball of three players.

A "four-ball" is a match in which two play their better ball against the better ball of two other players. It is a very popular form of play, and is often played among an informal foursome in conjunction with single matches, often on a Nassau basis.

The big equalizer in golf competition is its handicap system. Roughly speaking, your handicap is the number of strokes over par in which your average game is played. Let's assume your average score is 90 over a par-72 course. Your handicap would therefore be 18. Thus, in a stroke-play competition, eighteen strokes would be deducted from your score. In a match-play competition, you would deduct a stroke from your score on each hole. Should your handicap be less than 18—say 10—you would receive a stroke on every hole that is handicapped on the scorecard at 10 or less. These ratings are made according to the severity of the hole.

Golf is a game whose etiquette is strictly observed—or should be. As one of the oldest, most civilized pastimes ever devised by man, it has been kept that way mainly because of its strict code of politeness. Learn its etiquette, and you will enjoy the game all the more. Follow closely some procedures as recommended by the United States Golf Association:

(1). Do not move when a player is making a stroke.

(2). Do not talk when a player is making a stroke.

(3). Do not stand directly behind him or directly behind the hole when he is playing.

(4). Do not tee your ball until after your opponent or partner has played his shot and the ball has come to rest.

(5). Never play a shot until all players in front are well out of range. Even a ball that can't reach them can disturb them by its bounce.

(6). Keep track of when it is your turn to play. Then, hit the ball without delay.

(7). If you have lost a ball, signal the players behind to play through while you search for it.

(8). Smooth all footprints made in a sand bunker, either by using a rake or by sweeping your feet across the imprints.

(9). Divots—the slice of turf made by hitting a ball—should be carefully replaced and stamped down.

(10). Ball marks made on putting greens should be repaired with a wooden tee and stamped down by foot.

(11). Never place a golf bag on a putting surface.

(12). Hold the flagstick for your fellow-competitors by standing at arm's length from it.

(13). Never stand on the putting surface in another player's line to the hole.

(14). Be sure that the flagstick is always firmly replaced in the hole.

(15). Never drive a golf cart within 30 feet of a putting surface and never to within the confines of a hazard.

(16). Do not dally on the putting green after a hole has been completed.

(17). Always allow faster players to play through. If an empty hole lies ahead of you, invite the following players to play through whether they are faster or not.

(18). After you have holed out, remove the ball from the cup immediately. Golfers do not like to putt to a hole in which another player's ball is resting.

(19). Do not offer advice to another player unless it is solicited.

(20). When a man is playing with a lady partner, *he* should tee off *first*—the reverse of ordinary procedure. Since she will be using tee markers well in advance of his, he may accidentally hit her.

(21). Never let anyone under the age of sixteen drive your golf cart. It's no toy.

(22). Never walk off a putting green until all players putt out.

(23). When playing alone, give way to all matches. You have no standing on a golf course.

(24). Never play a practice shot. It is against the Rules.

(25). Learn the brand of ball you are playing before you tee off on the first hole. Should it be the same brand as another player's, make sure it has a different number.

2
The Clubs

THE IMPLEMENTS of golf are divided into two categories of clubs: woods and irons. The primary purpose of woods is to gain distance; the primary purpose of irons is to produce accuracy. But the longest wood player in the world is not a good one unless he can use woods with a certain degree of accuracy. And the straightest iron player in the world is not a good one unless he can hit irons with authority; that is to say, unless he can draw from each the forward thrust that has been built into it by the clubmaker. You can hit an iron string-straight, but the shot will be all but worthless if the ball drops 15 yards short of the flagstick. By the same token, a 300-yard drive is wasted if it lands in a hazard. Accuracy, then, is a concomitant part of woods and distance is a concomitant part of irons.

WOODS

In the now almost forgotten lexicon of golf, the first four woods were referred to, in the order of greatest distance, as the driver, the brassie, the spoon, and the cleek. Today, they are simply called the one-, two-, three- and four-wood, although most golfers still refer to their one-wood as a driver. In the past decade, the five-wood has come into favor. While most golfers think it is an innovation, actually it is a club that years ago was referred to as a baffy. It is an extremely valuable club for a beginner to concentrate on. Women seem to be particularly adept with it, which is not to imply that there is anything feminine about it. There are tournament professionals who swear by its efficacy.

The One-wood

The "driver"—or one-wood—is commonly used off the tees on those holes where distance is a major factor: par-fours and par-fives. For most men, the driver is expected to propel the ball somewhat in excess of 200 yards; for ladies, perhaps 30 yards less. Since the shaft on the driver is the longest among all clubs—usually 43 inches—and since the loft on its face is the shallowest, it is geometrically the most difficult club in the bag to play with accuracy. However, it is played to that area of the golf course that permits the widest margin for error—the fairway. Consequently, while accuracy is imperative on any drive, the degree of accuracy is nonetheless relative. You can hit a drive 20 yards off line, and still have hit a serviceable one.

The Two-wood

The two-wood, or "brassie," is constructed approximately along the same lines as a driver, except that it has more loft, thereby giving it an added degree of accuracy. It was orig-

34

inally designed to give the utmost distance off the fairway, when the ball must be played off turf rather than off a wooden tee. Notwithstanding, it's a club that requires considerable experience. As a result, it has within the past years come into disfavor among golfers, not coincidentally because the Rules of Golf limit the number of clubs you can legally use to fourteen. You might play ten rounds of golf and not find ten shots that call upon a brassie. So it often is thrown out of the bag to begin with.

The Three-wood

The part that the brassie used to take is today mainly taken up by the three-wood, or "spoon," one of the most utilitarian clubs in the bag. Most journeymen golfers can hit the three-wood in the neighborhood of 200 yards— ladies, proportionately less—and they employ the club with a degree of accuracy they often can't expect from their long-irons. They use it to approach the greens on long par-fours and for positioning the ball on second shots to par-fives. One of the truly great spoon players in the entire history of golf is Jack Nicklaus, who often uses his off the tee when he considers accuracy to be the better part of valorous distance. He loses some valuable yardage, but gains invaluable accuracy. Nicklaus, the strongest player in the game, knows that golf is basically a game of strategy, not muscle.

The Four-wood

The four-wood, or "cleek," is a spoon with additional loft. It substitutes for the three-wood when the ball is not lying in the fairway quite as cleanly as a lie from which you might expect to make a shot with the three-wood, or when the ball is lying in light rough and when distance is still an element. On occasion, you can extract from it practically the same distance as you can from a three-wood, although probably without any greater degree of accuracy. It is an extremely versatile club. It supplies the power of the three-wood with almost as much loft as a middle-iron. Down through the years the leading virtuoso of it has been Jimmy Demaret, who can command from it shots ranging all the way from 190 yards to 230 yards, depending upon the terrain, the velocity of the wind, and the instance of draw or fade he wants to apply to the ball.

The Five-wood

The five-wood, the historical "baffy," has a shorter shaft than the four-wood and as much more loft than the four-wood as the four-wood has over the three; but it can supply the utmost distance you can get from your longest iron while also giving out the loft you can extract from a shorter iron; say, your five-iron. Among average players, there are innumerable shots that will call for a five-wood.

In summing up, then, it may be said that your soundest combination of woods—taking into consideration the fourteen-club limit—is a driver, a three-wood, and a five-wood. The two-wood is a specialty club. The four-wood can replace the three-wood on occasion but cannot substitute for the five-wood. So stick to the one, three, and five.

IRONS

The basic list of irons stretches to nine. Historically, they were called the driving-iron, mid-iron, mid-mashie, mashie-iron, mashie, mashie-niblick, spade-mashie, spade-mashie-niblick, and niblick. (This nomenclature varied widely among clubmakers, however.) Today, you can ignore the names, none of which has been used in years by golfers. Some purists still refer to their nine-iron, with which they make most of their short approaches, as a niblick. But its role has largely been supplanted by a ten-iron and eleven-iron, which incongruously, still go by names: the pitching wedge and its father, the sand wedge, from which it derives so many characteristics. Strictly speaking, they are utility clubs but so useful that hardly anybody attempts to play golf without them any more. Their stroke-saving effectiveness in contemporary golf is beyond exaggeration.

The One-iron

The one-iron, or "driving-iron," is a club that nobody but an expert should attempt to use and hardly anybody but a touring professional actually can use. It has almost no loft and a shaft almost as long as a five-wood. With it, the ball must be struck with precisional timing beyond the means even of a scratch-player—and he would have to be playing almost daily golf to be sharp enough to bring it off with consistency. There are professionals who would not dream of carrying one in their bags. Its purpose is to hit the ball the same distance as a three-wood with a very low trajectory; for instance, in order to keep the ball low in a high wind that might very well blow a three-wood askew. Jack Nicklaus, as might be expected, is perhaps the leading exponent of it today. Since there are so few golfers who are vain enough to think they can play in his image, manufacturers do not even bother to make the club other than by special order. In short, now that you know what it is, forget it.

The Two-iron

A matched set of irons today traditionally begins with the two-iron, or "mid-iron." Because it, too, has a long shaft and very little loft, it remains the toughest club in the bag for the average player—which may explain why so many of them leave it out of the bag, also; the five-wood gets the same job done. Generally speaking, it releases the same distance as the four-wood but with a lower trajectory; again, it is used usually because of wind conditions.

The Three-iron

Now we get into the category of really useful irons for the average player. The three-iron, or "mid-mashie" as it used to be called, is very valuable because it is the first iron among the so-called long-irons that he can use with any sense of security. He needs the three-iron because its range, for him, is approximately 170 yards, the distance from which he can first begin to reasonably expect to hit a green and stay on it. Taking another situation into consideration, most par-threes are within the range of a three-iron. So he has his confidence in it to back him up. It may be that the most useful advice on the use of a three-iron (or any other iron) is to swing it as though it were a short-iron. That is to say, handle it in the same tempo. You cannot possibly add any more length to it than the manufacturer has built into it.

The Four-iron

The four-iron, or "mashie-iron," is your final break between the long-irons and the middle-irons. Its precise use is difficult to describe to a beginner. Suffice it to say, there will be any number of occasions when the three-iron will be too much club for the shot at hand and the five-iron not enough. Golf is inarguably a game of strategy. But it is a highly instinctive one, too. After some experience you will know when a shot calls for a four-iron instead of a three or five.

The Five-iron

The five-iron, or "mashie," is the cornerstone among a set of irons. Its range lies at about 150 yards—the average distance you will need to reach a par-four hole or a par-three hole on the average golf course. It has a degree of serviceability even beyond that, for it is the club you will most want to use when chipping off the surface of a green. Furthermore, since it falls midway in the spectrum of the irons, it calls upon the swing of which the swings on all other clubs are variations. You can do a whole lot worse than to practice it alone if your practice time is limited. Swing a two-iron in the same tempo you swing a five-iron or swing a nine-iron in the same tempo, and you can't go too far wrong mechanically. It may be a compromise, but you'll get results. The name of this game is score, not style. As Lloyd Mangrum used to say when he was criticized for his somewhat unorthodox methods, "What are we playing? How? Or how many?"

The Six-iron

As the four-iron is the final break between the long-irons and the middle-irons, the six-iron (the "mashie-niblick") is the break between the middle-irons and the short-irons. Its range lies in the neighborhood of 140 yards. Since so many factors other than distance have a bearing on your selection of clubs—the direction of the wind, the position of bunkers around the green, the elevation of the putting surface—again your knowledge of when to use a six-iron rather than a seven- or a five-iron will come largely from instinct, something that can be developed only through experience. Even then you will never be utterly sure. In fact, proper club selection is a problem no one ever thoroughly masters. Indeed, it seems to become more and more complex as your experience increases. As Bobby Jones once said, "Golf is the only game I know that becomes more difficult the longer you play it."

The Seven-iron

The seven-iron (the "spade-mashie") is the first of the so-called short-irons. Strategically, the short-irons are used when accuracy is almost entirely your purpose; which is to say, when reaching the green is no longer a problem. Your immediate concern now is hitting the green and placing the ball as close to the flagstick as possible. Short-irons must be hit smartly, to be sure, but they are swung at with something less than a full swing. You are playing what is known in golf parlance as an "approach." Consequently, there is no sense in hitting a nine-iron full when you have an eight-iron in your bag, nor any sense in playing an eight-iron full when you have a seven-iron.

The Eight- and Nine-irons

If the range of your seven-iron approximates 130 yards, then the range of your eight-iron (the "spade-mashie-niblick") can be expected to be 120 yards. (Roughly, there should be 10 yards' difference between all irons.) Within that area from 110 yards down, then, becomes the territory of your nine-iron, the ubiquitous "niblick," which many golfers use for any shots down to 40 yards and even for chips when little run on the ball is desired.

The Pitching Wedge

From about 80 yards down, however, most golfers rely heavily on the all-purpose "pitching wedge." It supplies the utmost in loft among the irons and, when struck properly, the utmost in backspin, thereby stopping the ball in the minimum amount of space, a condition that is paramount when the flagstick is placed in the vicinity of a hazard. The closer you get to a green, the more your pitching wedge will be called upon. While it must be played with authority, as any club should, it is nevertheless used on what might be looked upon as half shots or even quarter shots, the most delicate shots in the game. The master of this shot is Julius Boros, a golf pro built along the dimensions of a piano mover. Nevertheless, he can handle the wedge with the touch of a watchmaker.

The Sand Wedge

The "sand wedge" is a club developed not quite forty years ago. It has revolutionized scoring in golf. In the hands of a professional, it is, like the pitching wedge, a deadly effective weapon. Until the development of the pitching wedge, in the late forties, it was even used off turf, and still is by some pros on odd occasions. For your uses, however, it would be wise to confine its duties to sand bunkers. Get confidence in the sand shot, and you have gone a long way toward playing like an experienced golfer.

The Putter

This is a straight-faced club—one with very little loft—which is used to roll the ball along the ground.

A full complement of clubs, then—to summarize—would be the one-, three- and five-woods; the two- through nine-irons; both a pitching wedge and a sand wedge, and finally, of course, a putter, giving you a legal bag of fourteen clubs. All sorts of variations on this list are possible, though. Bandleader Fred Waring, a devotee of golf for half a century, uses no irons whatsoever, save for his sand wedge, which is the one indispensable iron in the bag. Waring uses twelve woods, all substitutes for every iron through the pitching wedge. While such a bagful of clubs is not advisable, particularly for a beginner, it shows that much is within the imagination of golf. Putting it another way, what makes golf golf is its infinite capacity for improvisation.

3
The Grip
and the Swing

THE GOLF swing is initiated by the combination of three physical attitudes. The first, and easily the most important, is the grip, or the placement of the hands on the club. The second is the stance, or the position of the feet on the ground. The third is the address, or the posture of the body in relation to the direction in which you want the ball to travel.

Once set in motion, the golf swing is composed of a long list of synchronized physical mechanics: straight left arm, cocked chin, steady head, square clubface, bent left knee, tucked right elbow, sliding hips, shoulders under, firm left side, follow-through and so on through a list that seems to grow lengthier and more confusing the longer you play the game. Most of them can be conquered, and consequently forgotten, by the use of native abilities you would apply to any physical maneuver—swimming, dancing, riding a bike—that requires balance, timing and rhythm. Almost every mistake you can make in the golf swing—slicing, hooking, topping and that horror of horrors, shanking—can be traced back to a lack of balance, timing or rhythm.

What makes the golf swing such a maddeningly confusing thing to get mechanically right is that not even championship golfers seem to agree on just how to go about it. Take the address. Three contemporaries—Sam Snead, Ben Hogan and Jimmy Demaret—all went about it in a different way. Snead aligned himself somewhat to the right of his target. Hogan was dead on line. Demaret aimed distinctly to the left of it. Notwithstanding, the ball as likely as not ended up the same place; which is to say, where their eyes were aiming.

Even on such an obviously important subject as timing there has always been wide disagreement. Such titlists as Cary Middlecoff, Tommy Armour and Walter Hagen had distinct pauses at the tops of their backswings. Jones, Hogan and Arnold Palmer had a noticeable lack of one. Indeed, Jones argued that the downswing began with the trunk of the body before the backswing had been completed with the hands and arms, thereby giving the illusion of a pause.

Whatever any good player does physically during the golf swing, he always has only one thing uppermost in mind while he does it: hitting the ball. "If I ever thought of anything else," Jones has said, "I didn't hit it."

One of the great theorists of the game was the late Ernest Jones (no relation to the famous Bobby). An Englishman who immigrated to the United States during the twenties after losing a leg in World War I, Jones went the great players one step more. The one categorical imperative in golf, he argued, was to hit the ball. But if you swung the clubhead, the ball would take care of itself.

Jones made his discovery soon after he lost his leg. Desperate to return to the game he loved and off which he had made his living as a professional before the war, he forced himself to devise some method of hitting the ball while balanced on the leg he had left. After some heart-rending falls, Jones through trial and error found out that he could keep his balance only when he concentrated hard on swinging the clubhead, dismissing everything else from mind. Furthermore, when he concentrated only on swinging the clubhead, all the mechanics of the swing seemed to fall into their rightful places. In other words, the mechanics of a golf swing were not the cause of a good golf swing but the results of it. Swing the clubhead, he reasoned, and you can forget about everything else.

Jones made a handsome living for nearly half a century expounding his theory to golfers who were suffering, as he termed it, from "paralysis by analysis." This is to say, they were ruining their golf swing by trying to divide it into the mechanical parts they thought made it up. "You can't divide a golf swing into parts and still have a golf swing," he said. "Look! If you dissect a cat, you've got blood and guts and bones all over the place. But you haven't got a cat."

To demonstrate what he considered to be the true swinging motion, Jones used to tie a penknife to the end of a handkerchief. Holding one end of the handkerchief between his thumb and his forefinger, he would swing the penknife back and forth, like a pendulum. Gradually lengthening the arc, he would point out that as long as he maintained the swinging motion the handkerchief would remain taut. Once, however, he attempted to add leverage—say, by jerking his hand—the handkerchief would collapse. Outside power, therefore, was not only superfluous but undesirable. No matter how hard you try, you cannot move a penknife on the end of a handkerchief—or move a golf club—any faster than you can swing it. Why, then, try to do anything else? "The golf swing is effortless power," Jones said, "not powerful effort."

"The golf swing is effortless power," master teacher Ernest Jones used to say, "not powerful effort." He demonstrated his theory by swinging a weight on the end of a string. Any unnecessary power collapsed the string, thereby ruining the swing.

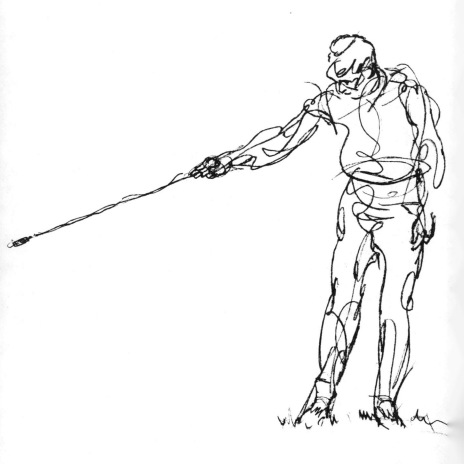

THE GRIP

The swing is begun by the hands. They have to begin it. After all, they are the only parts of the body attached to the club. By any consensus of any group of golf teachers, the single most important fundamental in golf is the manner in which the hands are placed on the club—the grip. The grip determines your authority over the clubhead, which in turn determines the behavior of the clubface, which determines the control of the ball.

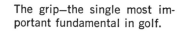

The grip—the single most important fundamental in golf.

There are some good golfers who employ unorthodox grips. But there are no bad golfers who employ an *orthodox* grip. Develop a sound grip, and all the other fundamentals of the swing fall into place.

By all odds, the most nearly universal grip in golf is the "Vardon," or so-called overlapping grip. It derives its name from Harry Vardon, an English professional who revolutionized golf form at the turn of the century. For seventy years it has proved to be the easiest way to hold on to the club as comfortably at the top of the backswing as at the beginning, without any loss of power or control at impact with the ball.

To the beginner, it seems an awkward way to hold anything, his natural tendency being to grab the club with his hands rather than grip it with his fingers. You need only hold the club in the palms of your hands baseball fashion to realize how little control you have over the clubface. Squeeze it till your hands turn white, and a child can still twist the clubface at will.

No, what is needed is control through the fingers without any sacrifice in the natural power of the hands. The Vardon grip is the most effortless way to go about it.

Any grip, whether it be the Vardon or not, requires the back of the left hand and the front of the right hand to be aimed toward the target and the palms of both to be in opposition with one another. In the Vardon grip the right, or lower, hand overlaps the left, but only in the sense that one finger overlaps it. This is to say, the little finger of the right overlaps the forefinger of the left.

This overlapping accomplishes two objectives:

(1). It helps to unify the hands, for golf is a two-handed game, with control derived mainly from the left and power mainly from the right, although each hand shares a measure of the other's responsibility.

(2). Overlapping permits only four fingers of the right actually to be on the club at once, thereby diminishing

The overlapping, or so-called Vardon, grip. The little finger of your right hand overlaps the forefinger of the left, thus unifying your hands. It is the most popular grip today.

the usually stronger right hand's tendency to overpower the usually weaker left.

The club is placed across the fingers of the left hand in such a manner that the pad of the hand rides atop it. Done properly, the club may be held at arm's length simply by crooking the forefinger underneath it without any help whatever from the remaining fingers. The thumb is then clamped to the top of the shaft and placed in such a way that a distinct groove is formed between it and the back of the hand. When the clubhead is laid on the ground, this groove should point somewhat to the right of your head— between it and your right shoulder.

The right hand is placed on the club much in the manner of shaking hands. As pointed out, the little finger overlaps the left forefinger, riding in the groove formed by it and the left middle finger. The club is then squeezed by the ring finger and the middle finger of the right hand, these two fingers being the chief sources through which the power of the right hand is transmitted. The thumb and the forefinger are then wrapped around the club until their tips touch, their primary role being to keep the clubface in proper position as it is swung through the backswing and then whipped through the ball.

It is only through such a grip that you can, with any effective consistency, swing the clubhead, whether your purpose be for a "chip" of 30 feet, a "pitch" of 30 yards or a "drive" of 300. No grip other than the Vardon, or a close approximation of it, allows for such diversity among so many different types of people, regardless of height, weight, strength or hand size.

If the hands are the only parts of the body attached to the club, it must be kept in mind also that the feet are the only parts of the body attached to the ground. They have their job to do, too. One sure way to keep them from doing it properly is to place them haphazardly as you step into the ball.

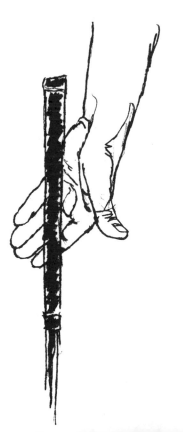

Any grip, including the Vardon, requires that the **back** of your left hand and the **front** of your right hand be aimed toward the target. The palms of the two hands are in opposition to one another.

The grip is first assumed with the club laid across the fingers and palm of your left hand.

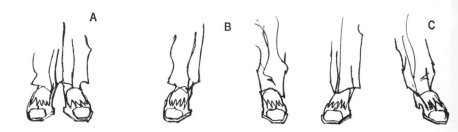

The position of your feet is assumed by (A) first placing them together, (B) spreading them apart about shoulder distance and (C)
finally turning your left toe slightly toward the target.

THE STANCE

A convenient method of learning how to place the feet
correctly is to check yourself on the linoleum or other
composition tiles usually used on bathroom or kitchen
floors. Any flooring will do, actually, as long as it has
parallel lines.

Holding your feet together as though at attention, spread
them evenly apart until each comes to rest on a line, about
the width of your shoulders apart. Your feet now run
squarely along the lines, neither flared out nor pigeon-toed.
Then, leaving the right as it is, turn the toes of the left
roughly 20 degrees to the left, in the direction in which
you want the ball to go. With the weight of the body
evenly distributed on both feet, as much on the heels as
on the balls of them, this is the basic stance for every shot
in golf.

There are ramifications of this stance, indeed; notably for putting, chipping and pitching. But these are mere sophistications of the basic stance, each designed to make the player more comfortable as less of his body is called into use. (In putting, for example, you don't use the body at all.) If need be, he could play any of these side shots from the basic stance. But he couldn't play a full shot from any of its ramifications.

Flaring the left foot out serves its purpose, and so does keeping the right foot straight. As the club is swung back, a firm support is needed to balance the weight of the body as the momentum of the clubhead forces it to pivot on the right knee, through the twisting of the hips and the simultaneous turning of the shoulders. This momentum also requires that the left knee tuck in so that it is pointing behind the ball, not stuck out so that it points in front of the ball. Tucked in in such a way, the left knee assists the right leg in supporting the weight of the body as the clubhead reaches the top of the backswing. Stuck straight out, it throws the preponderance of weight to the left leg, resulting in a multitude of sins, foremost among which is that you may miss the ball entirely—an error that counts just as much as a stroke as a shot you knock into the hole. In golf, a "stroke" is any motion made at the ball with the intent to hit it, regardless of the outcome. The drawings on pages 56 and 57 illustrate how your stance affects your swing.

Failure to point your left foot slightly toward the target has a tendency to bow your left knee straight out on the backswing, throwing the preponderance of your weight to the left side rather than "behind" the ball.

Keeping your right foot square to the line of flight gives you the support needed to balance the weight of your body as the clubhead forces it to pivot on your right knee.

THE ADDRESS

Having placed the feet properly on the ground, squarely along the desired line of flight, it becomes necessary to see that both the hips and the shoulders are also aligned squarely with the line of flight. There should be nothing difficult about this procedure, for, once the feet are square, you need only stand straight to have the hips and shoulders square also. However, since the shot is intended to go at right angles to the left, many golfers have a tendency to

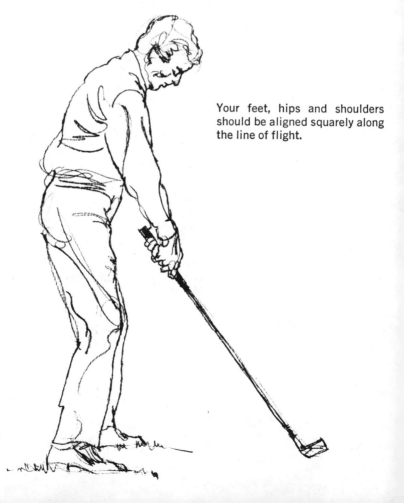

Your feet, hips and shoulders should be aligned squarely along the line of flight.

Chronic slicers have a tendency to turn the hips and shoulders toward the target, thereby throwing the clubhead outside the line of flight.

turn either their hips or their shoulders, or both, toward the target.

This is a particularly vicious habit among chronic slicers—those who have a marked peculiarity for hitting the ball with left-to-right spin on it. They do this because, having flared the hips and shoulders out of alignment, they throw the clubhead outside the line of flight, causing it to cross the ball from outside the line to inside it, thereby creating a shot much in the manner of a massé in billiards.

It is easily the most common fault in golf. Ninety-nine out of every hundred golfers err in this direction. The other 1 per cent have to fight a natural tendency to hook the ball; that is, hit it with right-to-left spin. It is a phenomenon of golf, though, that from this small minority come practically all the good players in golf. The hook, then, is the bane of the expert. It's the slice you will have to worry about.

One handy way to check the alignment of your feet, hips and shoulders is simply to stand in a doorway as though you were about to address a ball, your body aligned with the sides of the doorway. Holding the club, you now reach for the ball by flexing your knees, as though you were about to dive off the side of a swimming pool. Turning your head from right to left, you can inspect your hips and shoulders to see if you have any tendency to flare them toward the target. This is the posture you must assume on the golf course, adjusting your sight to the target from it. Simply because you can see the target is no guarantee of the shot's success. After all, there are blind golfers who bring off perfect golf shots. They do so because they have aligned their bodies properly.

Flexing the knees is an absolute in good golf form. It is the only method whereby you should reach for the ball as it lies on the ground. It should be done as though you were about to sit down but had changed your mind in the middle of doing so. There is no bending over at the hips. The back remains straight. The weight remains evenly distributed between the heels and the balls of the feet. There is no sense of squatting or crouching. Rather, there is a sense of unreleased energy in the legs. You should feel as though the knees, hips and shoulders may be turned at will in either direction. Should someone ask you a question when you are in such a position, you shouldn't feel as though you had to stand up to answer.

Once the clubhead is laid on the ground in this manner, there should be no reaching for the ball. The clubhead

Your knees should **not** be kept rigid, as above, but, rather, flexed, as if you were about to sit down.

There should be no sensation of reaching for the ball. Instead, the radius of your swing should be determined by a straight—but not rigid—left arm, and your knees should be flexed enough to allow the clubhead to reach the ground.

should fall directly behind the ball without any other effort. If it doesn't, the entire body—not just one part of it—should be shifted until the clubface is where it should be. How far the ball should be from you is determined by the left arm, which is extended without becoming rigid. Once the swing has been set in motion, it is the left arm that will determine the radius of it, allowing the clubface to return squarely back to the ball.

Since the right hand will be lower on the club than the left, it should be placed on the club by lowering the right shoulder. It should not be placed on the club by jutting the right shoulder out toward the ball. This action throws the shoulders entirely out of position. In point of fact, it puts them into the dreaded slice position.

One sure indication as to whether or not the stance is correct is the position of the hands at the address; or, more particularly, the position of the wrists. In other words, they are set in such a way that the club seems to become a straight extension of the arms. If there are wrinkles, this means the wrists are bent, thereby breaking the radius of the swing you want to establish with your left arm. In short, you are crouching.

Every shot in golf should be addressed in an attitude of calm expectancy. The body should be relaxed but not loose, firm but not taut. For, in essence, a golf swing consists of two motions: a backswing and a downswing. In the former, tension is built up. In the latter, it is released. In the former, energy is stored up by the muscles. In the latter, it is transmitted by the muscles of the body through the hands to the shaft out of the clubhead into the ball.

Many beginners, and not a few veteran players who never seem to improve, spoil this energy-building process by becoming overly tense before the swing has begun. They grip the club tightly in an effort to make it feel lighter than it is. Consequently, they fail to generate any tension during the backswing and so have no energy to deliver to the ball in the downswing.

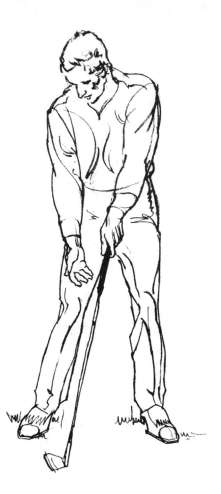

Your right hand should be placed on the club by lowering your right shoulder.

Do not place your right hand on the club by jutting your right shoulder out.

A golf club should never be gripped any tighter than you would shake hands with a lady. After all, a golf club weighs less than a pound, or less than a tennis racquet. Because most of its weight is concentrated in the head, however, it should feel heavier than it actually is. It is this feel of the clubhead that permits you to generate clubhead speed, that permits you to swing the club rather than merely hit with it. Remember, it is physically impossible to move the clubhead any faster than you can swing it—which helps explain why golf is almost unique among sports in that a good little man is at no disadvantage at all with a good big man. On anybody's list of the ten greatest players in the history of the game, not more than one of them stood more than 5 feet 11 or weighed more than 190 pounds.

The Waggle

Unnecessary tension in the address can be dissipated through what is known as the "waggle." This is a preliminary motion—a kind of swing in miniature—during which you imitate the path you want the clubhead to follow during the first 2 feet of the backswing.

It is done entirely by the hands and wrists. The wrists are cocked backward and forward, but not up and down, as the clubhead describes the first 20 degrees or so of the arc you want it to take when you initiate your backswing.

In addition to relieving tension, the waggle helps to establish the tempo you want to maintain throughout the entire swing.

Additionally, it serves as a double check on your distance from the ball. As the clubhead is waggled back and forth, the center of the clubface—the "sweet spot"—should return precisely to the belly of the ball. The sweet spot is where the weight of the clubhead is concentrated and, hence, is where the preponderance of the club's mechanical energy is stored.

66

Unnecessary tension in the address can be dissipated through
what is known as the "waggle."

The waggle is done by the hands and wrists, which are cocked backward and forward preliminary to making your actual backswing.

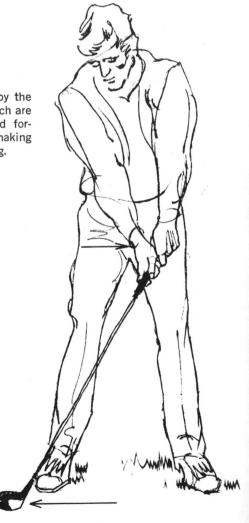

THE BACKSWING

The backswing evolves out of the motion established by the waggle. This is to say, you should go directly into the backswing from a series of waggles without pausing. Keep uppermost in mind that the backswing is just that: a swing. It is not a lifting action or any other type of action. It is a swing pure and simple, something that cannot be seen or photographed or described in words. You can only feel it.

Two things mechanical are of great aid in making sure the golf swing is a swing throughout its entirety. They are a sure grip on the club and a stationary head position. You should be distinctly conscious of the hands on the club throughout the entire swing, even when they are behind your head. And your head should feel as though it were suspended in space.

This feeling is particularly crucial at the start of the downswing, which is a stage when many golfers have a tendency to duck their heads in an often disastrous effort to elevate the ball. All the loft necessary for any golf shot has been built into the clubface. All you can do is move the ball forward. While the head may move back and forth to a degree, it must not be permitted to move up or down. Moving it up causes you to top the ball, moving it down causes you to hit behind the ball, among other things. If the head is held relatively stationary, you should be able to see plainly the dimples on the ball throughout the entire swing.

While the backswing is initiated by the hands—and followed in turn by the arms, shoulders and hips in natural anatomical order—it is accomplished by all these factors working in unison. Ideally, the shoulders should turn twice as far as the hips. Theoretically, although sometimes impossibly for physical limitations, the shoulders should turn a full 90 degrees, while the hips should turn 45 degrees.

69

While the backswing is initiated with your hands—followed in turn by your arms, shoulders and hips in natural anatomical order—it is accomplished by all these factors working in unison. Ideally, your shoulders should turn almost twice as far as your hips.

In the backswing the muscles, stretching from a relaxed position, store up energy.

This position places the hands just behind the right ear, the left shoulder just under the chin. The weight of the body should now be braced by the right leg, which is still in the flexed position it was at the address, and is supported by the inside of the left foot, particularly by the joint of the big toe.

At the top of the backswing, a distinct feeling of unreleased tension should be felt in the shoulders, particularly along the left shoulder and through the left arm. Somewhat less tension should be felt in the hips, but it should be distinct nonetheless, particularly in the left hip. It is the unleashing of this tension that will initiate the downswing, in a manner that is almost entirely instinctive.

THE DOWNSWING

The downswing, of course, is the backswing in reverse anatomical order. Therefore, it is initiated by the hips. While the hands are held stationary somewhere in the vicinity of behind the right ear, the left hip is twisted back toward the target so that the left heel returns precisely to the position it was at the address. As the hips pass a line parallel to the intended line of flight, the shoulders, in natural order, begin to turn toward the target also. They, in their turn, pull the arms and hands down parallel to the ground. All this has been accomplished without any conscious throwing of the hands or arms toward the ball. The feeling is almost as though the club had purposely been left at the top of the backswing. You can't actually do this, of course, but that is nevertheless the feeling. It is the trunk of the body that has done all the work, instinctively unleashing all the tension that has been built into it by the backswing. You have arrived at the moment of truth in the golf swing.

The weight of your body has been returned almost completely to the left side. It is braced by the left leg, which

In the downswing the muscles transmit energy through your hands to the shaft out of the clubhead into the ball.

is still in the flexed position it was at the address, and is supported by the right foot, particularly by the joint of the big toe—just the reverse of the position on the back-swing. The right knee has been tucked in toward the left knee and is already well past the ball. The head is still stationary. The hands are at hip level. The shaft of the club is parallel to the ground.

At this stage, you have generated so much motion—swinging motion—that only a conscious effort can disturb the clubhead from striking the ball in the manner you had acted out with the preliminary waggle. You need only swing *through* the ball. There is no necessity to swing *at* it.

There is a long list of "don'ts" associated with arriving at the moment of truth in the downswing. Chief among them would be:

(1). Don't try to throw the clubhead at the ball with your hands from the top of the backswing. If you do this, you succeed only in throwing it outside the line of flight, resulting in either a slice or a darting hook, the former caused by an open clubface and the latter by a shut club-face. Furthermore, you dissipate a great deal of clubhead speed.

(2). Don't try to help the ball into the air.

Both of these errors—and a lot of others—can be eliminated by two positive movements:

(1). Leave the clubhead at the top of the backswing until the weight of the body has been shifted to the left side, spinning the left hip out of the way. By leaving the club-head behind you, so to speak, until the preponderance of your weight has shifted to the left side, the clubhead remains inside the intended line of flight until impact.

(2). Consciously tuck the right knee toward the left knee well in advance of hitting the ball. By tucking the right knee toward the left before you make impact, you have eliminated any tendency to keep your weight on your right side, which is the only position from which you can, consciously or unconsciously, scoop the ball into the air.

Even if, by accident, you make solid contact with the ball by scooping it, at best you have only succeeded in turning a five-iron, say, into a six-iron. And what is the point in that?

THE FOLLOW-THROUGH

The finish of the golf swing—the "follow-through"—obviously contributes nothing toward hitting the ball, since the ball is well on its way by the time you arrive at the follow-through. But the correct follow-through serves its purpose nevertheless.

All truly polished players are conspicuous for the gracefulness of their follow-through. Their weight is perfectly balanced on the left leg, they are standing in an upright position, the hands are high above the head, the right arm extended, the left tucked into the side. They have been able to arrive at this position because everything that preceded it was executed correctly. If they don't arrive at this position, they check backward to try to find out what went wrong.

Let's assume, for instance, that the bulk of the weight still remains on the right leg instead of the left. This result would be impossible had you tucked the right knee toward the left before you hit the ball.

Or let's assume, on the other hand, that the hands have finished low—say, somewhere in the vicinity of the left shoulder. They could not have finished in this position if the clubhead had been left at the top of the swing when you initiated the downswing with the left hip.

And on it goes. The correct follow-through is the result of a correct downswing. If it is incorrect, check backward to find out why.

At the finish of the follow-through, you should return to a nearly upright position, your weight balanced mainly on your left leg, your right arm almost extended, your left arm tucked into your side.

PITCH SHOTS AND CHIP SHOTS

Pitch shots and chip shots are golf shots in capsule form. Since they are played from distances downward from a hundred yards to a matter of only feet, their primary purpose is accuracy.

Consequently, a pitch is played with a backswing only three-quarters or half as long as normal, depending upon the distance desired. While the standard address is used, the stance finds the feet played much more closely together, since little or no shifting of weight to the right side will be required on the backswing.

Notwithstanding, there must be the distinct sensation of moving to the left side on the downswing. The club-head must be felt as though it were being left behind as the left hip moves past the ball. And the right knee should tuck in toward the left before contact is made with the ball.

All this is as it would be with any golf shot. Golfers who fail to execute these two movements have a tendency to "wheel" on the ball with a pitch; which is to say, they lock their hips and throw the clubhead outside the line of flight. The result is that they often "blade" the ball in a sort of roundhouse action or hit it cleanly without benefit of backspin.

The pitch is more often than not played with the pitching wedge, the most lofted club in the bag. People who never seem to get the knack of pitching are people who never put complete faith in this loft. They invariably try to hit the ball higher than the clubface will permit it to go, resulting in the uncontrollable shots described above. Therefore, think only of hitting the ball forward and let the clubface get it into the air for you.

The chip shot is a miniature form of the pitch. Its purpose is to loft the ball over a few feet of fairway or rough until the ball bounces on to the putting surface,

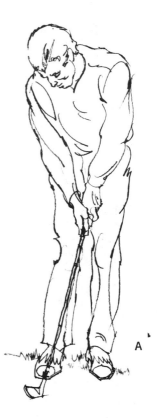

A

A. The chip is a pitch shot in miniature, addressed with your feet close together, your hands well down on the shaft.

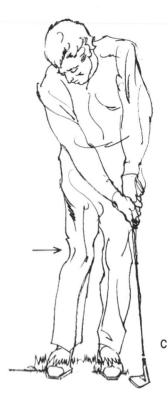

B. The backswing is slight, and is accomplished solely by your hands and arms.

C. The shot is struck crisply, again with little or no body movement, although your right knee should be permitted its natural tendency to tuck in toward your left knee.

thereafter running to the hole in the manner of a putt. It should be played with practically no body action to speak of, although again the right knee should be allowed to tuck into the left as you swing through the ball.

Although pitches and chips are to be played purely for accuracy's sake, they must nevertheless be executed with authority. They should be hit briskly, with the arms and hands, although power is not at stake. If not, the ball is without backspin, or without control, and will not have the braking power to stop on a putting surface. Regardless of how close you are to the flagstick, be firm with the shot.

The most popular grip with the putter is known as the "reverse overlap" grip. All the fingers of your right hand are placed on the club. The index finger of your left hand overlaps two fingers of your right hand.

PUTTING

Putting is the most highly instinctive form of golf there is. Almost nobody can teach someone else to putt. Putting is largely a case of developing a comfortable style, and will be as individualistic as your handwriting.

While most golfers err in their shots by trying to add loft to the ball, they usually err in their putts by trying to hit the ball into the green rather than roll it over the green. This is best accomplished by forcing yourself, regardless of what type of stroke you use, to keep the clubhead as

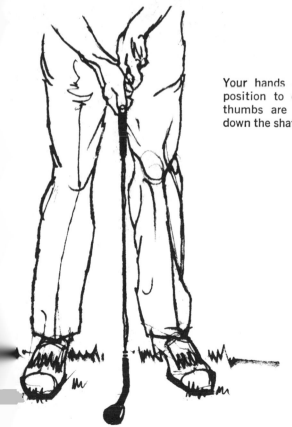

Your hands are in direct op-position to one another; the thumbs are pointing directly down the shaft.

close to the ground as possible throughout the entire stroke.

One aid toward this end is to alter your grip until the palms are opposed to each other with the thumbs pointed straight down the shaft. With the hands in this position, most top players further alter their grips by reversing the overlap. This is to say, they overlap one or two fingers of the right hand with the left index finger, rather than have the little finger of the right hand overlap the left.

So that is the game of golf—perverse, infuriating and wholly satisfying. It now remains only to play the game.

Glossary of Golf Terms

Ace. Slang for hole-in-one.

Address. The position in which a player puts himself in order to strike the ball.

Approach. The placement or attempt at placing the ball on the putting green.

Away. A player whose ball lies farthest from the hole is said to be *away.*

Baffy. The number-five wood.

Bent. A finely textured species of grass used for putting greens.

Bermuda. A coarsely textured species of grass in which the strands intertwine. Used for both fairways and putting greens, especially in hot, humid climates.

Best-ball Match. One in which one player competes against the better ball of two other players.

Birdie. A hole scored in one stroke less than par.

Blind. A term describing a hole when its green cannot be seen by a player as he approaches.

Bogey. In America, a hole played in one more stroke than par. In Great Britain, the number of strokes a better-than-average player is expected to take for a hole.

Brassie. The number-two wood.

Bunkers. Obstacles at the edges of the fairways and the approaches to the putting greens.

Caddie. A person who carries the player's clubs.

Carry. The distance between where a ball is hit and where it first strikes the ground.

Championship. A tournament representing title to a trophy offered for competition, usually annually, by a recognized golfing body, such as the United States Golf Association or the Royal and Ancient Golf Club of St. Andrews, Scotland. The Open and Amateur Championships of these organizations are recognized throughout the world as the major championships of the game.

Chip. A short approach consisting almost entirely of run.

Cleek. The number-four wood.

Course. The terrain over which play is permitted.

Cross-bunker. A narrow bunker that crosses a hole at a right angle to the player's line of fire to the putting surface.

Cuppy. A lie in which the ball is positioned in a small depression in the ground.

Dead. A ball so near the hole that the holing of the putt is a certainty.

Divot. A piece of turf sliced while playing a stroke.

Dog leg. A hole whose fairway is marked by an acute bend.

Double-eagle. A hole played in three strokes less than par. (A par-five in two strokes is very rare.)

Draw. A slight hook in the flight of a ball.

Driver. The number-one wood.

Driving iron. A hickory-shafted, flanged iron with approximately the loft of a contemporary number-one iron.

Eagle. A hole played in two strokes less than par on a par-four or par-five.

Face. The surface of the club with which the ball is struck.

Fairway. The expanse of ground between the teeing ground

and the putting green, which is especially prepared for play.

Flagstick. A movable indicator centered in a hole to show its position on the green.

Flash trap. A small, shallow sand bunker.

Flat. A very obtuse angle between the sole of a club and the shaft. Also the characteristic of a player whose swing is not considered upright.

Follow-through. The continuation of the swing after the ball has been struck.

Fore! A cry of warning to other players or to spectators.

Four-ball match. One in which two play their better ball against the better ball of two other players.

Foursome. A match in which two play against two, each side playing one ball in alternate strokes. (This is not four-ball.)

Green. The whole course, particularly a surface especially prepared for putting.

Grip. The part of the shaft that is held in the hands. Also the grasp itself.

Half-shot. A shot played with less than a full swing.

Halve. A hole is said to be halved if each side holes out in the same number of strokes.

Handicap. The number of strokes over par in which one's average game is played. This number may be deducted from that player's actual score in a match play competition.

Hanging. A lie in which a ball is situated on a slope inclining downward.

Hazard. An area, such as a bunker or a pond, in which the privileges of play are restricted.

Head. The part of the club distinguished from the shaft.

Heel. The part of the face of a club nearest the shaft.

Hole. In general, the part of the course from the tee to the putting surface. Also the circular opening, or cup, in the green into which the ball is played. It is 4¼ inches in diameter.

Hole-in-one. A hole scored in two strokes less than par on a par-three.

Hole out. To make the stroke that puts the ball into the cup.

Honor. The privilege of playing first from a tee, which cannot be declined.

Hook. To hit the ball with a right-to-left spin.

Hosel. The socket into which the shaft of an iron is fitted.

In. A term referring to the second nine holes of a golf course, as opposed to "out," the first nine.

Irons. Clubs with metal blades for heads. Today, most irons are made of chrome-plated carbon steel.

Lie. The state of the ball's position on the ground.

Line. The direction in which the player intends the ball to travel after it is hit.

Links. Originally, a course laid out on linksland, the sandy soil deposited by centuries of receding oceanic tides. Today it has become a synonym for any golf course.

Loft. Any angle less than 90 degrees on the face of a club. Also, to hit the ball with a high trajectory.

Lofter. A form of hickory-shafted niblick or other highly lofted iron.

Marker. A scorer in stroke play who is appointed by the tournament committee to record a competitor's score. He may be a fellow-competitor. He is *not* a referee or a forecaddie.

Mashie. A hickory-shafted iron with approximately the loft of a present-day number-five iron.

Mashie-iron. Either a mashie with a longer shaft or a hickory-shafted number-four iron.

Mashie-niblick. A hickory-shafted number-six iron.

Match. A contest between two players, or between a player and a side, or between two sides, which is determined by the number of holes won and lost.

Match play. A tournament or championship conducted under the Rules of match rather than those of stroke play.

Medal. The low qualifying score for a match-play tournament or championship. Also, slang for a stroke-play competition.

Mid-iron. A hickory-shafted number-two iron.

Mid-mashie. Either a deep-faced mashie or a hickory-shafted number-three iron.

Nassau. Three matches in one. One point is allotted for the first nine holes, another point for the second nine, and still another for the over-all eighteen.

Niblick. Depending upon the period referred to, any short, stiff iron with more loft than a mashie. Used for getting the ball out of bad lies. In the twenties, it had the loft of a present-day number-nine iron.

Odd, the. A stroke more than the opponent played

One-wood. The driver, commonly used off those tees where distance is a major factor.

Out. A term referring to the first nine holes of a golf course, as opposed to the second nine.

Par. The number of strokes an expert golfer is expected to make on each hole. It is determined by the length of the hole, although configuration and the severity of hazards has a bearing. A par-three is any hole up to 250 yards. A par-four is any hole between 251 and 470 yards. A par-five is any hole longer than 470. (For women these yardages run from 40 to 70 yards less.)

Pitch. To lob, or loft, the ball into the air.

Pitch-and-run. A shot so played that part of the desired distance is covered by the roll of the ball after it strikes the ground.

Pitching wedge. The iron with the most loft, good for short, high shots.

Pot bunker. A small, deep sand trap.

Pull. A wide, pronounced hook.

Push. A shot that travels on a straight line but well to the right of the intended line.

Push shot. A stroke with an iron designed to keep the ball long and low to the ground, popular in the day of the hickory shaft. The player keeps his weight well on his left side and then hits the ball with a sharp, descending blow. An effective shot in a high wind.

Putt. Any short stroke in which the ball rolls along the ground. Usually confined to specially prepared greens.

Putter. A straight-faced club, or one with very little loft, with which the ball is putted. Usually the last club used on each hole.

Rough. The part of the course that is not tee, fairway, green or hazard.

Rub of the green. Any chance deflection of the ball while its in play.

Run. The distance the ball rolls after striking the ground.

Run-up. An approach in which the ball travels close to or on the ground.

Sand wedge. An iron that is used to extricate the ball from sand.

Scratch. In America, to play at par. In Great Britain, to play at bogey.

Scratch player. A player who needs no handicap.

Scruff. To cut just through the roots of the turf in playing the ball.

Shaft. The part of the club that is not the head.

Shank. The part of the hosel nearest the face. Also, to hit the ball on the shank.

Short game. Pitching, chipping and putting.

Side. The player or players forming one part of a match.

Single. A match between two players. Often erroneously used in reference to one player who has no standing on a golf course.

Slice. To hit the ball in such a way that it has left-to-right spin. (The opposite of *hook*.)

Socket. The opening in the neck of an iron club into which the shaft is fitted. Also, in Great Britain, to shank a shot.

Sole. The bottom of the club on which the club rests when placed in position on the ground.

Spade-mashie. The first of the "short-irons." A contemporary number-seven iron.

Stroke. A forward movement of a club, made with the intent to hit the ball. Whether successful or not, it counts.

Strokes play. A competition in which the player's total score for the round is compared with the scores of other players in the field.

Swing. The sweep of the clubhead in the operation of hitting the ball.

Tee. The wooden peg on which the ball is generally placed for the first shot to each hole.

Teeing ground. A limited, marked place outside of which it is forbidden to drive the ball.

Three-ball match. One in which three players compete against each other, with each playing his own ball.

Threesome. A match in which one player competes against two others of a side, the two playing alternate strokes with the same ball.

Three-wood. The spoon.

Through the green. Conditions governing play from the time the ball is played from the tee until it reaches the green, with the exception of hazards but not the rough.

Top. To hit the ball above its center.

Tournament. A competition at either match or strokes play. A tournament is said to be "open" when both amateurs and professionals may participate.

Up. A hole, or holes, to the good of an opponent.

Upright. The angle between the head of a club and its shaft that is less obtuse than a flat lie. Also, the characteristic of a player's swing.

Whipping. The thread or twine used to wrap the area where the head and shaft of the club are joined together.